Usborne

First Magic Painting
Garden

Designed and illustrated
by Emily Beevers

Dip the brush into water, then
sweep it across each picture to see
the paint magically appear.

Use the flap at the
back of the book to
stop the paint from
seeping through to
the next page.

A furry
fox

A buzzing
bumblebee

A leafy tree

A fluffy squirrel

A fluttering
butterfly

A bright sunflower

A wiggly
caterpillar

A busy
bird

A croaky frog

Beautiful
flowers

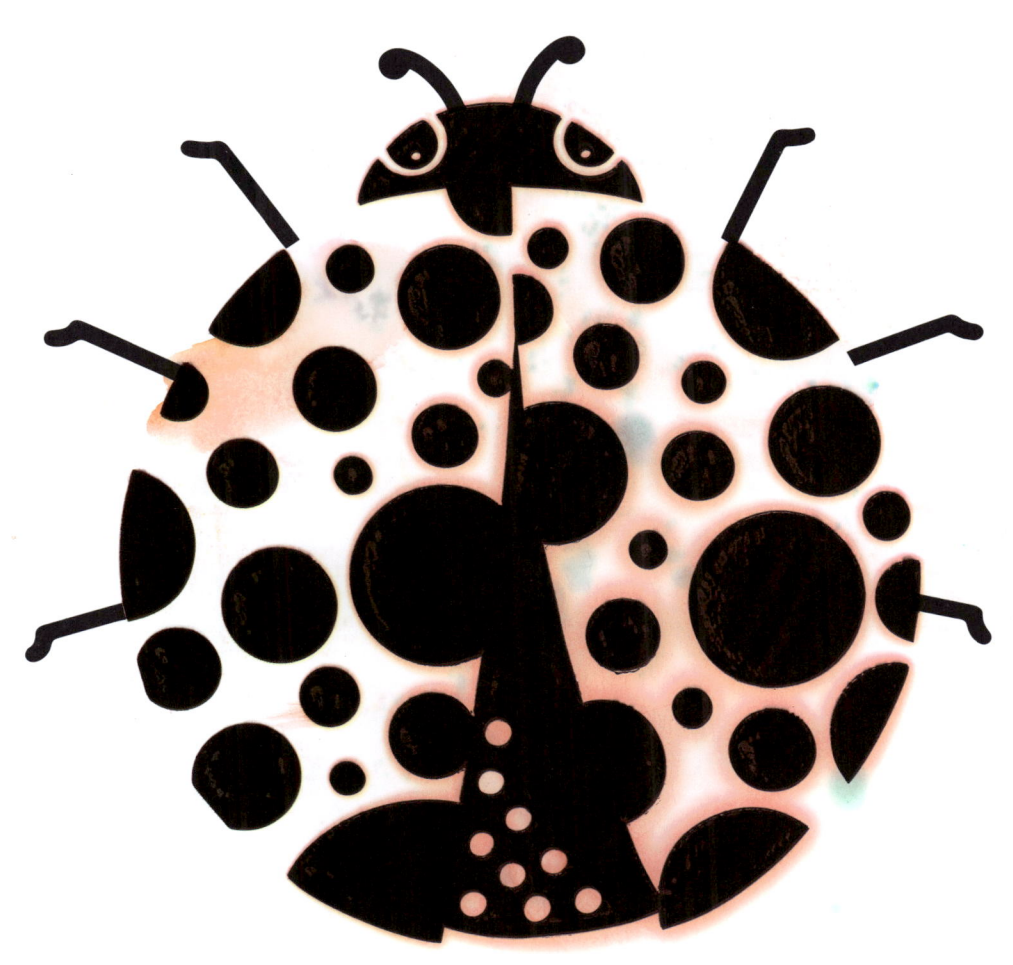

A spotty
bug

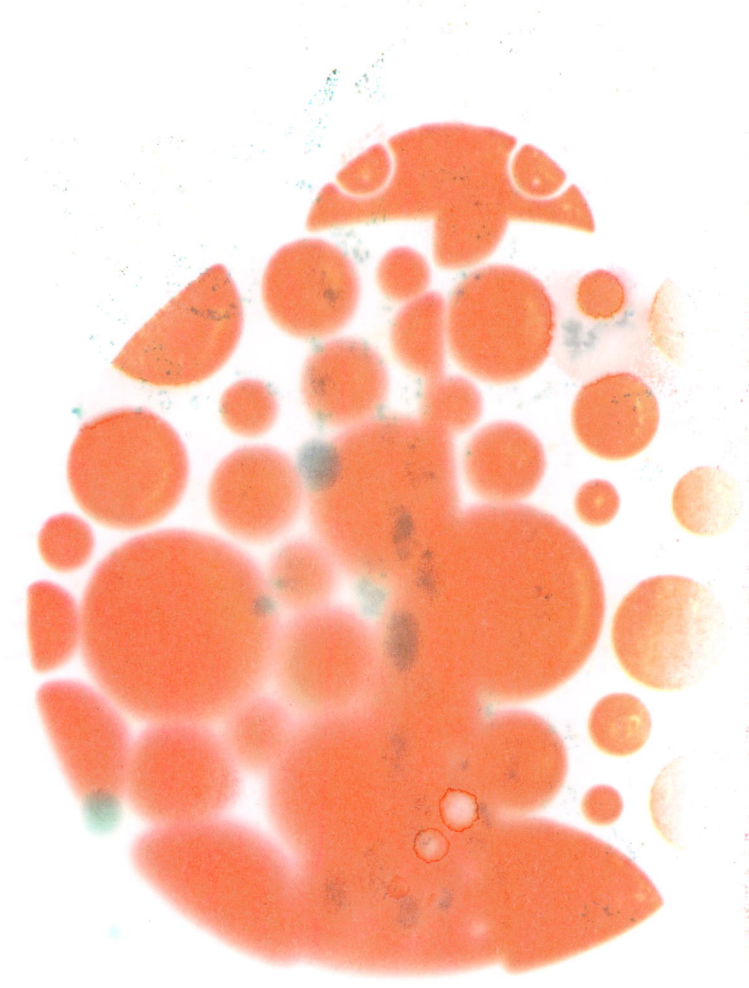

A prickly
hedgehog

A slow snail

A friendly fish

Tall tulips